THE QUEEN'S DIAMOND JUBILEE YEAR

A ROYAL SOUVENIR

ANNIE BULLEN

DUNDURN

TORONTO

Contents

Jubilee Highlights

4 FEBRUARY – 26 OCTOBER
60 Photographs for 60 Years, an exhibition of photographic portraits of The Queen, on display at Windsor Castle

6 FEBRUARY
The 60th anniversary of Her Majesty's accession to the throne

8 MARCH–25 JULY
The Queen and the Duke of Edinburgh make a series of regional tours of the United Kingdom, to celebrate her 60-year reign.

12 MARCH
The Queen attends a Jubilee Commonwealth Day Observance Service in Westminster Abbey

20 MARCH
The Queen addresses Lords and Commoners in Westminster Hall and re-dedicates herself to the service of her people

5 APRIL
The Queen celebrates the Royal Maundy at York Minster

25 APRIL
Her Majesty names the Royal Rowbarge *Gloriana* on the River Thames and visits Greenwich to unveil the restored *Cutty Sark*

9 MAY
The State Opening of Parliament and The Queen's Speech

10–13 MAY
The Diamond Jubilee Pageant at Windsor Castle

14 MAY
New figure of The Queen unveiled at Madame Tussauds in London

19 MAY
The armed forces march past and muster at Windsor Castle

22–26 MAY
The Chelsea Flower Show, at the Royal Hospital, Chelsea

29 MAY
The Buckingham Palace Garden Party

2 JUNE
The anniversary of The Queen's Coronation; Her Majesty attends Derby Day at Epsom racecourse and begins the major Jubilee celebrations

3 JUNE
The Jubilee Pageant on the River Thames; The Queen's barge is accompanied by a flotilla of 1,000 small boats; street parties and community celebrations are held throughout Britain

4 JUNE
A spectacular concert and a big picnic are held at Buckingham Palace; over 4,000 fires and beacons are lit around the world in celebration

5 JUNE
A service of Thanksgiving is held at St Paul's Cathedral, and a carriage procession to Buckingham Palace, a 60-gun salute, a fly-past and a 'fire of joy'; the Royal Family appear on the balcony of Buckingham Palace

16 JUNE
Trooping the Colour, on Horse Guards Parade marking The Queen's official birthday

18 JUNE
The Ceremony of the Order of the Garter, at St George's Chapel, Windsor

19–23 JUNE
The Queen attends Royal Ascot, in Berkshire

30 JUNE–8 JULY
The Queen's diamonds are on display at Buckingham Palace (and 31 July–7 October)

2–6 JULY
Holyrood Week and the Royal Garden Party at Holyroodhouse, in Edinburgh

The Diamond Queen

The year 2012 sees the United Kingdom celebrating not only Her Majesty's Diamond Jubilee but also the country's hosting of the Olympic Games, the world's greatest sporting event.

Visitors flocked to Great Britain, many making for London, England's historic capital city where The Queen and her family have their official residence, Buckingham Palace. The Queen, born in London on 21 April 1926, grew up in the city and has seen its iconic buildings, from ancient Westminster Abbey and Wren's St Paul's Cathedral, joined by modern wonders, from The Shard and the 'Gherkin' to the greatly admired Tate Modern, the London Eye and the reconstructed Shakespeare's Globe. Some of these magnificent buildings and monuments are the settings for many of the State occasions in which The Queen plays the leading role, while all attract visitors to the city.

The State Opening of Parliament in the Palace of Westminster, Remembrance Day at the Cenotaph in Whitehall and Trooping the Colour on Horse Guards Parade, Whitehall are just some of those occasions when London, transformed by the brilliance of ceremony, is shown at its sparkling best.

The Queen and her consort, Prince Philip, Duke of Edinburgh, carry out ceremonial duties such as the Royal Maundy in cathedrals thoughout Britain, while the ancient Ceremony of the Garter is held annually at St George's Chapel, Windsor.

Those who came to London to celebrate the Diamond Jubilee of the best-known woman in the world, enjoyed not only the glittering pageantry for which Britain is deservedly famous, but also a beautiful city, modern and vibrant in outlook and with a long and enthralling history.

Commonwealth Day

'We share one humanity and this draws us all together,' The Queen told the billions of people who belong to the Commonwealth, of which she is the Head. The message came in March 2012, during a Jubilee Commonwealth Day Observance Service when she was joined by the Duke of Edinburgh, the Prince of Wales, the Duchess of Cornwall and the Countess of Wessex in historic Westminster Abbey.

The service had 'Connecting Cultures' as its theme, for the 54 nations that belong to the organization. 'Connecting Cultures' ... encourages us to consider the special opportunities we have, as members of this unique gathering of nations, to celebrate an extraordinary cultural tapestry that reflects our many individual and collective identities,' said The Queen.

Before the service soprano Laura Wright, accompanied by Reading Blue Coat School Choir, gave the first public performance of *Stronger as One*, a Commonwealth anthem written specially for the Jubilee celebrations.

Commonwealth stars took part, including Canadian singer Rufus Wainwright, who gave a rendition of the Leonard Cohen anthem *Hallelujah*, and South African trumpeter, 72-year-old Hugh Masekela.

Queen & Country

Members of both Houses of Parliament gathered in Westminster Hall, in March 2012, to mark Her Majesty's Diamond Jubilee. Her address, in which she praised Parliament as 'an unshakeable cornerstone of our constitution and our way of life', received a standing ovation.

The Queen noted that since her accession she has had dealings with 12 Prime Ministers, had signed more than 3,500 Bills into law, and was 'merely the second Sovereign to celebrate a Diamond Jubilee' – a reference to her great-great-grandmother Queen Victoria. She also took the opportunity to re-dedicate herself to the service of 'our great country'.

During the ceremony a Diamond Jubilee stained-glass window, a gift from both Houses of Parliament, was unveiled. Designed by John Reyntiens, it contains 1,500 pieces of glass and will be installed above the North Door of Westminster Hall.

The World Comes to Windsor

Performers from the Commonwealth and around the world put on their dancing shoes and saddled up their horses to pay homage and to entertain Her Majesty The Queen. As Head of Commonwealth, she has made 250 visits to its 54 countries since her accession to the throne in 1952.

Windsor Castle was the venue, over three nights in May 2012, for a spectacular 90-minute show performed by more than 1,000 dancers and singers and 554 horses, from the Royal Canadian Mounted Police (the Mounties), Oklahoma Cowboys and Russian Cossacks, to the Royal Cavalry of Oman and Marwari dancing horses of India. The Windsor Pageant was the curtain-raiser for the showpiece Jubilee celebrations.

Her Majesty and the Duke of Edinburgh were guests of honour on the final night of the show when stars, including singers Susan Boyle, Joss Stone, Rolf Harris and Il Divo, joined the Commonwealth performers. Other singers included the Nairobi Chamber Chorus and the Watoto Children's Choir from Uganda. Dancers from Mexico dressed in brilliant colours, sword-bearing Te Awara Maori performers and sparkling Cook Island dancers brought glamour and excitement to the show, while folk musician Raghu Dixit, classical violinist David Garrett and Nashville singer Abigail Washburn entertained in style. The seven acts of the show featured the countries to which Her Majesty has made State and Commonwealth visits.

A Dance Extravaganza

The Queen and the Duke of Edinburgh arrived at the final performance on the third night of the Diamond Jubilee Pageant, with its fabulous stage built to resemble Buckingham Palace, by horse-drawn carriage (see pages 16–17). The royal performance was hosted by Dame Helen Mirren and Alan Titchmarsh.

Also enjoying the daring equestrian manoeuvres and glittering entertainment were the Princess Royal, the Duchess of Cornwall, the Duke of York, Princess Beatrice, and Prince and Princess Michael of Kent.

At a tea party before the show, Her Majesty tried on a pair of African bracelets, made for her as a Jubilee gift by

Kenyan tribespeople. The royal party were entertained by some of the world's finest equine talent, brought together in spectacular style. The troupes, from the prancing and dancing Marwari horses, decorated with silver, jewels and bells, to the Chilean cowboys (*huasos*) with their well-trained steeds, performed with breathtaking virtuosity.

Italy's Carousel of the Caribinieri re-enacted the 1848 *Charge of Pastrengo* in a flurry of swords and feathers, while horsemen from Russia's Kremlin Riding School gave a daring display of mounted acrobatics. Her Majesty also enjoyed lively and expressive performances from men and women drawn from nine Kenyan tribes.

All the Queen's Men & Women

More than 2,500 members of the armed forces paid a Jubilee tribute to their Commander-in-Chief as they paraded and mustered at Windsor Castle in May 2012.

Accompanied by six military bands, members of the Royal Navy, the Army and Royal Air Force formed into a parade half a mile long, taking 15 minutes to march past The Queen, who has taken a keen interest in her armed forces since being appointed honorary Colonel of the Grenadier Guards when she was 16 years old.

The colourful parade, their entry heralded by a fly-past of nine RAF Typhoons in the 'Diamond Nine' formation, marched closely past The Queen in Windsor Castle Quadrangle, before moving through the town of Windsor, watched by a 20,000-strong crowd. The services personnel mustered in a specially built arena in the Home Park,

where they were joined by The Queen and the Duke of Edinburgh, who were cheered by well-wishers as they travelled by car through Windsor.

An invited audience of almost 4,000, including several members of the Royal Family, visiting sovereigns and heads of state, service veterans and family members, were gathered.

A drumhead service, where a makeshift altar is formed by three tiers of drums, took place before the Chief of the Defence Staff, General Sir David Richards, paid tribute to The Queen: 'For six decades, your devotion to duty, sense of honour, and pride in our country have set the standards to which your armed forces constantly aspire,' he said from a podium in the arena.

The servicemen and women took their hats off to Her Majesty as they gave a resounding 'three cheers'.

Saluting the Sovereign

Tradition has it that the armed forces pay Jubilee tributes to their monarch, with similar events having taken place for Queen Victoria and King George V in the past. The Queen reviewed each of the services separately for her Silver Jubilee in 1977 and attended a tri-services event in Portsmouth for her Golden Jubilee in 2002. The parade and muster in Windsor Home Park 2012 was the first time all three services have visited The Queen for such an event.

Her Majesty, who watched the brilliant ceremony at Windsor with evident enjoyment, told the gathering that it was a tradition of very long standing that the Sovereign and members of the Royal Family were intimately associated with the armed forces, and had been proud to serve in all three services. She was referring to the fact that her father, husband, three sons and two of her grandsons had all served (or are still serving) in the armed forces. She paid tribute to all those brave men and women serving today: 'We are very proud of the selfless service and sacrifices made by servicemen and women and their families in recent years.'

'It is very gratifying to celebrate and take pride in successful achievements, but the real test of character is the ability to maintain morale and a positive spirit in bad times as well as when things are going well,' said The Queen from the grandstand.

The muster closed with a spectacular fly-past of current and historic aircraft, led by a magnificent Lancaster bomber and four Spitfires, from the Battle of Britain Memorial Flight. The air display included the number '60' formed in the air by Tucano training aircraft flying in tight formation. Chinook combat and reconnaissance helicopters also took part, while the Red Arrows concluded the display with a colourful sweep over Windsor Castle.

A Day at the Races

The Queen spent the first day of the official Jubilee celebrations, in June 2012, doing what she loves best – enjoying a day at the races. Derby Day at Epsom Racecourse has been attended by Her Majesty regularly since her Coronation in 1953 and this, her Diamond Jubilee year, saw her arrive in a motor cavalcade with the Duke of Edinburgh by her side. The royal party included the Duke of York, his daughters Princess Beatrice and Princess Eugenie (below, far right), and the Earl and Countess of Wessex. Earlier, gun salutes sounded across London and other parts of the United Kingdom, to mark the start of the celebrations and the 59th anniversary of The Queen's Coronation.

As Her Majesty and her consort were driven slowly around the racecourse, 130,000 flag-waving spectators, led by soprano Katherine Jenkins, sang the National Anthem while the Red Devils army parachuting team, trailing coloured smoke, landed with precision on the grounds.

The Queen, who once said that if she were not destined to wear the crown, she would like to be a lady living in the country, surrounded by animals, is passionate about horse racing and rarely misses the Derby, or Royal Ascot. She toured the parade ring to inspect the runners before watching the favourite, Camelot, ridden by Joseph O'Brien, come from behind to win the most historic and famous race in the world, renamed The Diamond Jubilee Coronation Cup for the occasion.

Although Her Majesty, who is an acknowledged expert in judging and assessing racehorses, did not have a runner in this year's race, she looked relaxed and happy. Wearing a white and blue silk dress under a royal blue wool coat with a matching hat, she watched intently and with obvious enjoyment.

The River Thames Pageant

The Queen and people everywhere smiled and waved at each other throughout the day, almost without a pause, in the greatest spectacle the River Thames has seen in Her Majesty's 60-year reign.

Dressed in a stunning gold-and-silver-spotted white coat and dress, embellished with glittering crystals, the Sovereign showed the same Dunkirk spirit as more than a million of her subjects lining the riverbanks and those taking part in the spectacular 1,000-vessel flotilla on a cold, wet day in June 2012.

However, although the light was grey, the mood of the crowd was bright, as the tremendous procession with The Queen's magnificent barge, *Spirit of Chartwell* (below right), at its heart, made its stately way along the river.

The pealing Jubilee bells on the floating bell-tower, aboard a barge leading the flotilla, were echoed by churches throughout London; orchestras played, singers sang, and whistles and hooters added to the celebration, as her people cheered, waved a million Union flags and roared their heartfelt good wishes to their Diamond Queen.

Her Majesty and the Duke of Edinburgh arrived at Chelsea Pier to be greeted by the Prince of Wales and the Duchess of Cornwall, a fanfare from six Royal Marine trumpeters and an honour guard of 22 Chelsea Pensioners (right) in their immaculate scarlet uniforms.

In what must have been a nostalgic moment for The Queen, the royal party was taken by the tender that once served the Royal Yacht *Britannia* to join *Spirit of Chartwell*, where the Royal Standard fluttered as they stepped aboard to join the Duke and Duchess of Cambridge. Splendidly liveried Royal Watermen were in attendance as The Queen surveyed the scene around her and declared it 'Spectacular!' Protected from the worst of the weather by an elegant glass canopy, she waved at the excited crowds.

Queen of the River

The gilded and flower-bedecked royal barge *Spirit of Chartwell* waited at her mooring as the first section of the seven-mile long pageant slipped past, each of the 260 small, hand-powered craft paying tribute to The Queen with cheers and salutes. The first vessel, a 12-tonne floating belfry with its eight specially cast Jubilee bells in full peal, seemed not in the least incongruous heading the magnificent procession.

Gloriana, the royal rowbarge, named for the spirit of the two great Elizabethan ages and presented to Queen Elizabeth II as a Diamond Jubilee gift, followed at a steady four miles an hour. Decorated with glittering gold leaf and built in the style of 18th-century royal barges, *Gloriana* carried 10 flags, among them those representing the four home nations, England, Scotland, Wales and Northern Ireland, as well as the flag of the City of London and that of Cornwall. The 18-strong crew was headed by Olympic gold medallists Sir Steve Redgrave and Sir Matthew Pinsent. In *Gloriana*'s wake followed the small and colourful craft, each powered by oars or paddles. (see pages 28–29).

The valiant fleet of hand-powered boats, which included Venetian gondolas, a Maori war canoe, dragon boats and the sea cadets' tiny craft bearing flags of all the Commonwealth countries, passed *Spirit of Chartwell*. Then all eyes were on this handsome ship of state as she slipped her moorings to take her place in the historic flotilla. Behind The Queen's barge sailed the Royal Squadron with the rest of the Royal Family.

Not since 1662, when King Charles II fêted his new bride, Catherine of Braganza, with a river pageant, has there been such a spectacle on the Thames, whose waters were calmed and slowed for the Diamond Jubilee by the closure, for the day, of the flood barrier.

Singin' in the Rain

Nowhere was the Dunkirk spirit more evident on the River Thames pageant than with the appearance of the next section of the flotilla. Several lovingly maintained craft that had taken part in the evacuation of Dunkirk in 1940 sailed past proudly. The Dunkirk 'Little Ships', joined by lifeboats and fireboats spraying celebratory water jets, touched a patriotic chord with the crowd, now 20-deep on the riverbank.

There was music, joy and laughter. There were cheers and tributes and fun along the pageant's seven miles. Her Majesty beamed with delight as Joey – the life-sized puppet from the West End hit play *Warhorse* – galloped on to the roof of the National Theatre to rear in salute, while dancers positioned themselves along the rooftop of the Royal Festival Hall to signal 'Happy Diamond Jubilee' in semaphore. Ten music barges, carrying bands and orchestras, slotted in between narrowboats and barges, tugs, cutters, smacks, luggers and motor-cruisers.

The London Philharmonic Orchestra barge, bringing up the rear, broke into the James Bond theme tune as it floated past MI6 headquarters and later, teased the rain-sodden crowds with a spirited version of *Singin' in the Rain*. Its heroic choir, from the Royal College of Music, who were soaked to the skin by the pouring rain as they floated past The Queen's barge, gave the performance of their lives with a joyful rendition of *Land of Hope and Glory* that rang out from riverbank to riverbank.

As the royal barge prepared to pass under London's iconic Tower Bridge, before mooring near HMS *Belfast*, a fanfare sounded and the two bascules on the bridge rose in full royal salute. The magnificence of the enormous flotilla combined with the joyous sense of a heartfelt tribute. Her Majesty watched it all and smiled. Crimson-draped thrones had been prepared aboard the royal barge but she and the Duke of Edinburgh stood for the whole proceedings, which had indeed been happy and glorious.

Britain Celebrates!

Buckingham Palace was the spectacular backdrop for a concert with stellar performances from some of the biggest stars from the years of The Queen's reign. Her Majesty made her entrance in time to see tenor Alfie Boe and soprano Renée Fleming sing a duet from a balcony on Buckingham Palace. She acknowledged happily the 500,000 concert-goers who had already enjoyed pop from singers including Jesse J and Will.i.am (right, inset), concert organizer Gary Barlow, Cheryl Cole and Tom Jones.

Dressed in a black evening cape over a gold cocktail dress covered with crystals, which sparkled in the evening sunlight, The Queen joined Prince Charles and the Duchess of Cornwall, the Duke and Duchess of Cambridge and Prince Harry in the royal box.

Pageantry and pop combined as the band of the Coldstream Guards opened proceedings with a drum roll and fanfare to back concert-opener Robbie Williams, singing, appropriately, *Let Me Entertain You.*

Buckingham Palace roof was the stage for the band Madness (right), singing their signature tune *Our House,* while other artists sang from a 360-degree stage.

Stars including Cliff Richard, Elton John, Annie Lennox, Shirley Bassey, Paul McCartney and Stevie Wonder paid tribute to The Queen as 18,000 guests cheered from their seats and thousands more watched on giant screens in The Mall.

As the concluding fireworks blazing into the night sky died away, Prince Charles paid tribute to his mother (below) and to his father, Prince Philip, who was unwell and unable to be with The Queen.

'I was three when my grandfather George VI died and suddenly, unexpectedly, your and my father's lives were irrevocably changed … this is our opportunity to thank you and my father for always being there for us. For inspiring us with your selfless duty and service and for making us proud to be British,' he said.

Picnics, Parties & Beacons

Streets, parks and village playing fields the length and breadth of Britain were a sea of patriotic red, white and blue as people everywhere celebrated with picnics, street parties and events to commemorate the Diamond Jubilee. Bunting, tablecloths, paper hats, napkins, flags, cakes, plates and mugs decorated with Union flag colours were brought out, as her subjects raised their glasses to toast The Queen. Many had gone the extra mile, wearing outfits to match the festive mood.

Church bells rang out from county to county, while musical entertainers broke into impromptu versions of the National Anthem.

At Buckingham Palace, 12,000 picnickers sat on The Queen's lawns to enjoy a five-course hamper meal devised by celebrity chef Heston Blumenthal and featuring chilled summer soup, Coronation chicken and Eton mess pudding. Most people had won their tickets to the picnic and concert in a public ballot, although 2,000 of the guests were invited representatives from charities supported by the Royal Family.

Around the world, beacons were being lit, blazing a trail that would lead to the heart of London. The first to be lit were those in Tonga and New Zealand, while Australian Prime Minister Julia Gillard set off the trail of fire in Canberra.

At least 4,200 fires blazed across the globe, 2,000 of these in the United Kingdom including beacons on landmarks and hills such as the peaks of Scotland's Ben Nevis, Snowdonia in Wales, Scafell Pike in Cumbria and Slieve Donard in Northern Ireland.

Closer and closer to home they came until, after the last notes of the Jubilee concert had died away, The Queen placed a cut glass 'diamond' into a wooden cradle to trigger the mechanism which lit the final dramatic beacon in The Mall, shooting flames 15 feet (4.6 metres) into the air.

Thanksgiving

Sixty years of sovereignty and service were celebrated by a multi-faith congregation at St Paul's Cathedral (below) on 5 June 2012, the final day of the long Jubilee weekend. For Her Majesty, who stepped from the royal car to loud chants of 'God Save The Queen!' from well-wishers gathered outside, this was the most profound event of the Jubilee.

Fanfares from the State Trumpeters heralded her arrival as she was greeted by the Lord Mayor of London, Alderman David Wootton, and led inside the great West Door of St Paul's Cathedral by the Dean, the Very Reverend Dr David Ison. In the absence of the Duke of Edinburgh, Her Majesty sat with other members of the Royal Family for the thanksgiving service.

Wearing a pale mint-green outfit of fine silk tulle, embroidered with tiny star-shaped flowers, she joined Prince Charles, the Duchess of Cornwall, the Duke and Duchess of Cambridge and Prince Harry, who had arrived a little earlier. The Princess Royal, the Duke of York (below, far right, with Prince Charles) and the Earl and Countess of Wessex (below right) also attended the service.

The Archbishop of Canterbury, Dr Rowan Williams, in his sermon said that in all her public engagements The Queen had shown a quality of joy in the happiness of others and had been generous in showing honour to countless local communities and individuals of every background, class and race.

'She has made her public happy and all the signs are that she is herself happy, fulfilled and at home in these encounters,' he said.

Her Majesty watched and listened with obvious enjoyment as a 'Diamond Choir' of 41 young choristers, hand-picked for the occasion, sang a new anthem, composed for her by Will Todd. The words to *Call of Wisdom* were written by Canon Michael Hempel. Following the service, The Queen attended a reception at Mansion House and a lunch at Westminster Hall with 700 guests invited by the Livery Companies of London.

'Fire of Joy' Salute

Her Majesty smiled broadly as a magnificent fly-past of 18 historic and modern aircraft, and a rarely performed rifle salute (below right) brought the official Jubilee celebrations to a sparkling end. The thousands thronging The Mall cheered themselves hoarse as The Queen, flanked by Prince Charles and the Duchess of Cornwall, the Duke and Duchess of Cambridge and Prince Harry, waved from the balcony of Buckingham Palace, the climax of four days of spectacle and fun.

The red-uniformed Irish Guards who had performed the *feu de joie* – an infantryman's historic rifle salute – with perfect timing, dropped to one knee to place weapons on the ground, before rising to their feet and lifting their bearskin caps high in the air to give three rousing cheers to their Queen. The crowd roared too, in appreciation of this remarkable woman who has become, above all, a symbol of dedication and duty to her subjects.

Earlier, thousands more of her subjects had waved and cheered as The Queen, leaving Westminster Hall, where she had attended a lunch with the City of London Livery Companies, stepped into the open top 1902 State Landau drawn by magnificent grey horses, wearing scarlet mane dressings. She was accompanied by the Prince of Wales and the Duchess of Cornwall (below) and was given a full Sovereign's Escort by the Household Cavalry Mounted Regiment (right) in their gleaming breastplates and plumed helmets. The Duke and Duchess of Cambridge followed in another State Landau, as the timeless and magnificent pageantry of a British ceremonial occasion brought enthusiastic approval from her subjects, each wanting to play their own part in saying 'thank you' to a Diamond Queen.

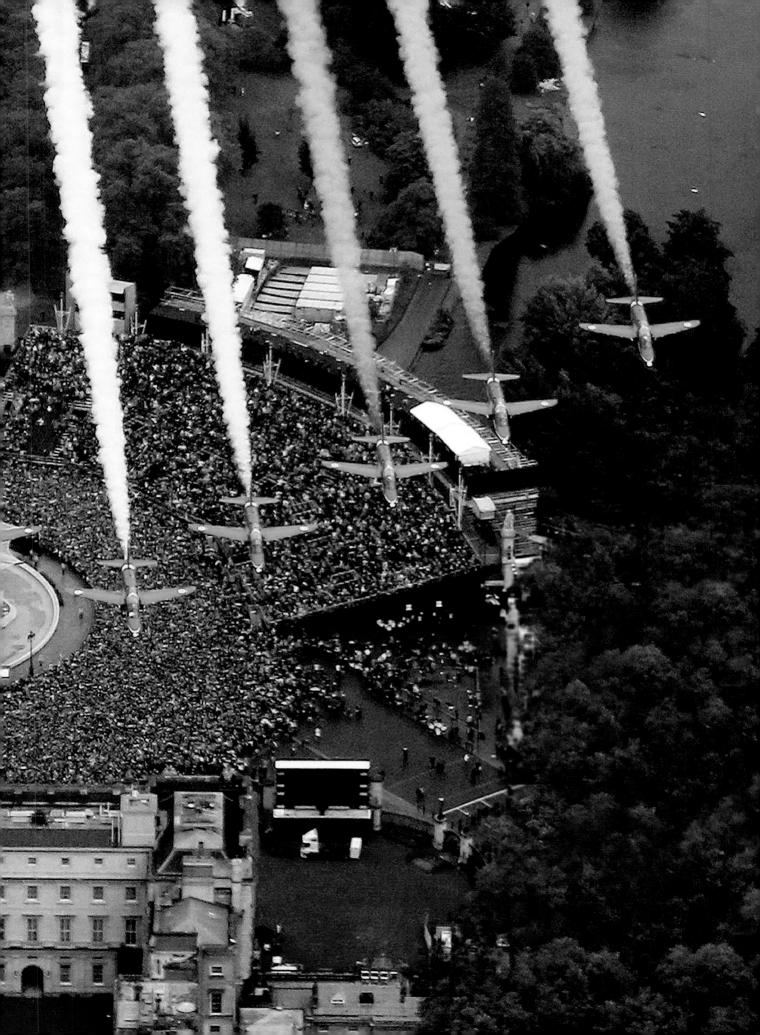

Leicester

The Queen embarked on a Jubilee tour of the United Kingdom in March 2012, to enable herself and the Duke of Edinburgh to meet as many of her subjects as possible.

The first visit was to Leicester, where Catherine, Duchess of Cambridge accompanied her grandmother-in-law (right) to a fashion show at de Montfort University, where Catherine was asked to choose her favourite pair of shoes from student designs. The winning pair, by young designer Becka Hunt, were to be made up for the Duchess. At the cathedral The Queen received several bunches of flowers from young admirers, while Catherine was handed a red rose – for Prince William. Leicester marked the Jubilee by asking The Queen to unveil a plaque for the newly named Jubilee Square in the city.

Manchester & Salford

The new BBC headquarters in Salford were the focal point of the royal visit to Manchester, where The Queen and the Duke of Edinburgh were given a tour of the studios in the MediaCityUK complex, before Her Majesty opened the high-tech new centre.

The royal couple delighted a pair of newly-weds, John and Frances Canning, whose marriage at Manchester Town Hall coincided with the official lunch. The Queen and Prince Philip shook hands with them, wished them the very best of luck and posed to have a photograph taken with the happy couple.

Later The Queen admired a giant throne, carved from a fallen beech tree, and now the centrepiece of the city's new Jubilee Garden.

North London

The Queen shared a joke with a 14-year-old schoolboy when she visited the 17th-century Valentine Mansion in Redbridge, north London. She and the Duke of Edinburgh had viewed paintings by celebrated British artists Lucian Freud, Francis Bacon and David Hockney, and then met artist Jason Rose who was painting a portrait of his teenage son, Alex, in the lobby. Her Majesty stopped to ask young Alex why he was wearing his school uniform and they laughed together when he told her: 'I managed to get the day off school because I told them I would wear my uniform!'

During her visit to north London (far right), The Queen enjoyed lunch at Waltham Forest and, in Walthamstow, met British kickboxing champion Ruqsana Begum, one of the Olympic Flame torch bearers.

Cutty Sark, Greenwich

On the morning that The Queen launched *Gloriana*, the £500,000 rowbarge at the centre of the Jubilee celebrations, she was reminded of what was probably her first ever engagement – the official opening of the world's last remaining tea clipper, the 143-year-old *Cutty Sark.* At the National Maritime Museum in Greenwich, she was shown footage of that occasion, in April 1937, when as an 11-year-old schoolgirl, she accompanied her father, King George VI, who had acceded to the throne the previous year when his brother, Edward VIII, abdicated.

Now the ship, which had been under wraps since its extensive damage in a fire in 2007, has undergone a £50 million restoration and The Queen unveiled it once again, in front of admiring crowds. After viewing the elevated vessel from the outside, Her Majesty went aboard to inspect the cramped decks which once would have been filled with tea chests.

The Queen was shown around the magnificent clipper by Richard Doughty, Director of *Cutty Sark.* Lord Stirling was there too, to admire the tea clipper, a living testimony to the glorious days of sail and, in her time, acknowledged as the fastest and greatest sailing vessel in the world.

South Wales

A thanksgiving service in Cardiff's Llandaff Cathedral was the first Jubilee engagement in South Wales for The Queen and Prince Philip, who arrived in the city by royal train. The Archbishop of Wales, Dr Barry Morgan, praised The Queen's commitment to public life.

'Over the last 60 years, amidst all the shifting sands of public opinion and different viewpoints, you have regarded the Christian faith as the rock on which you have been able to draw strength and comfort,' he said.

The next stop was to meet the Welsh rugby team, who won the 2012 Grand Slam and The Queen enjoyed a chat with the players (below right) before travelling to Merthyr Tydfil's Cyfarthfa Castle, home to the local High School. There she was serenaded by a talented singer, Tom Hier.

Her Majesty has shown continuing support for the village of Aberfan and on day two of her Welsh tour, she unveiled a plaque marking the opening of the new Ynysowen Community Primary School here.

At Ebbw Vale the royal couple talked to former steelworkers and attended a service at Christ Church, where The Queen addressed the community, praising the 'remarkable spirit of Wales': 'I have travelled the length and breadth of this country during my 60 years as your Queen. Prince Philip and I have shared many of the joys and sadnesses of the Welsh people in that time and have always been struck by your sense of pride and your undimmed optimism. That remarkable spirit of Wales has been very evident in this valley today,' she told the congregation.

Later she visited Glanusk Park where she planted a tree and enjoyed demonstrations of rural sports and country life, including sheep-shearing.

South-West England

When the royal train pulled in at Sherborne station, the first stop on a tour of the south-west, The Queen was greeted by well-wishers and their corgis, her favourite breed of dog, making her feel instantly at home.

She received flowers from eight-year-old Leah McGarry dressed as Alice in Wonderland, as she visited a Mad Hatter's tea party outside Sherborne Abbey, before enjoying a local produce fair and a 1952-themed coffee morning with guests from residential homes across Dorset.

Then it was back on the royal train bound for Salisbury, and lunch at The Rifles Regimental Museum, before a tour of the Cathedral Close, where The Queen enjoyed a series of medieval-themed activities from falconry to maypole- and morris dancing, and a display of treasures from communities across Wiltshire.

On the second day, the first stop was Yeovil, to be greeted by schoolchildren and taken to Nine Springs Country Park, where a Jubilee country fair was in full swing (far right, above). Her Majesty was delighted to meet and name two

police horses – Jubilee and Harry Patch – the latter title a tribute to the last British 'Tommy' to serve in the First World War trenches. The veteran soldier Harry Patch died in 2009, at the remarkable age of 111.

Flags were flying at Crewkerne Town Hall on the next stage of the trip. Then The Queen and the Duke of Edinburgh travelled to Exeter, where they visited Princesshay, a part of the city named specially after her in 1949 when, as the young Princess Elizabeth, she went there to mark the beginning of its redevelopment. As they arrived at Exeter University a special fanfare, written by the Musical Director Marion Wood, greeted the royal couple who were guests of honour at a Devon-themed lunch in the Great Hall after watching music and theatre performances by students. They were welcomed by university Chancellor Baroness Benjamin, a former children's television presenter. Later The Queen opened the new £48 million Forum Centre.

The Royal Family's Tours

Prince Harry's Tour

While The Queen and Prince Philip toured Britain to meet as many of her subjects as possible during Jubilee year, other members of the Royal Family undertook overseas visits.

The Queen's grandson Prince Harry was, for the first time, her representative abroad during a Jubilee tour of Belize, The Bahamas and Jamaica. He also visited Brazil in support of his African charity, Sentebale, where he enjoyed a game of touch rugby and a polo match (right, above and below).

The 27-year-old Prince, who revealed that his grandmother had told him to enjoy himself and to make her proud, said that he had been touched by his warm reception and by the way the countries were celebrating The Queen's 60-year reign.

In Belmopan, Belize's capital, Prince Harry named the new Queen Elizabeth II Boulevard and took part in a street party where, in a carnival atmosphere, he enjoyed local food, drink and music – and demonstrated his dancing skills. Later, he met children and visited a Mayan temple.

He joked, in a speech, that he was sorry the people were being visited by him, rather than The Queen: 'She remembers so fondly her visits to this beautiful realm and speaks of the warmth of welcome she received on her most recent visit... I'm only sorry she can't make it and you're stuck with me,' he said.

In Nassau, the Prince spoke to citizens telling them how much his grandmother loved their island.

'The Bahamas holds a special place in Her Majesty's heart,' he told the people.

'Her love for this realm and you, the Bahamian people, stretches back over the decades, right to that first visit in 1966. I am greatly looking forward to the next 24 hours and the chance to explore and meet more of the people of these stunning islands.'

'I'll certainly be showing off about it to my brother and sister-in-law when I return home,' he added. Later he visited tiny Harbor Island, where he was greeted by tourists and locals. The following day crowds of enthusiastic schoolchildren performed for Prince Harry in groups representing their schools, clubs and associations.

'It is clear to me that the young people of The Bahamas are living up to the country's motto – forward, upward, onward, together,' Prince Harry told them, before befriending 12-year-old Anna Albury. Anna, who is blind, sat next to him at the youth rally and made a stirring speech, encouraging other young people to pursue their dreams, for which she was congratulated by the Prince.

At a reception for youth leaders, Prince Harry met a beauty queen, invited because of her charity work. The reigning Miss Bahamas, Anastalgia Pierre, 23, had professed her intention to ask the Prince to marry her, but when the time came, her nerve failed.

Prince Harry in Jamaica

In Jamaica, in March 2012 Prince Harry triumphed by sprinting to a finishing line ahead of Usain Bolt, the world's fastest man – but only by jumping the gun. The fun race was pre-arranged – although the Prince's crafty strategy was not! But Olympic gold-medallist sprinter 'Lightning' Bolt, took Prince Harry's ploy in good heart, roaring with laughter at the royal ruse and slapping him on the back.

On a visit to Rise Life, an organization for deprived young people in Kingston, the Prince was invited on to the floor by dancer Chantal Dormer (see page 54),

and showed great style as he moved, wearing blue suede shoes, to a version of the Bob Marley reggae classic *One Love*.

Prince Harry's easy style with its blend of informality and charisma served him well and was well-received everywhere on his first solo visit overseas – and will have earned his grandmother's approval.

Later he confessed that the experience had been an emotional one and that at times he had felt 'choked up' by the reception he had received. The warmth of the reception 'has been utterly amazing,' he said.

The Princess Royal in South Africa

While Prince Harry represented The Queen in Belize, the Bahamas and Jamaica, his uncle, Prince Edward and wife Sophie, the Earl and Countess of Wessex, visited other destinations in the Caribbean (and, later, Gibraltar) in her name, as did the Duke of Gloucester, The Queen's cousin, who made a Jubilee visit to Malta. The Princess Royal, Princess Anne, travelled to South Africa, attending engagements in Pretoria, Johannesburg and Cape Town, also visiting the Soweto Equestrian Foundation, where children from the Adelaide Tambo School demonstrated their riding skills for her. Her brother, Prince Andrew, Duke of York, paid a seven-day visit to India. The Duke of Kent visited Uganda and the Falkland Islands. The host countries each held events to mark the visits.

Royal Visits to Canada

The Royal Family has always had a special relationship with Canada, particularly since the month-long visit made to the country by The Queen – then Princess Elizabeth – and Prince Philip in October 1951.

They were representing King George VI, her father, who was too ill to travel. The young couple enjoyed the 10,000-mile coast-to-coast trip; as ball followed banquet, presentations and speeches were made, the famous Calgary stampede was inspected and square-dancing in Rideau Hall, Ottawa was clearly a high-point.

Similarly the newly-married Duke and Duchess of Cambridge, The Queen's grandson, Prince William and his wife Catherine took Canada to their hearts on their first visit there together in 2011. Canada reciprocated, giving the young couple a rapturous welcome. Catherine was spotted wearing a maple-leaf brooch, belonging to her grandmother-in-law and given to The Queen as a present on an earlier trip.

Charles & Camilla in Canada

The Prince of Wales and his wife Camilla, Duchess of Cornwall carried on the tradition of close links with Canada, paying a Jubilee visit in late May 2012, arriving at New Brunswick's St John Airport on a Royal Canadian Air Force Airbus. Prince Charles, paying his sixteenth visit to the country, spoke of his days as a young naval pilot on exercise in Canada, 37 years ago, when he spent five weeks living in a tent at the Canadian Forces base, Gagetown.

The Prince described his joy at travelling back to the country to celebrate his mother's Diamond Jubilee and told an audience of Forces families, dignitaries, including Canada's Governor-General David Johnston, Heritage Minister James Moore and war veterans:

'I am delighted that my wife and I are beginning this, my sixteenth, visit over the past 40 years to Canada here in Gagetown, where I have fond memories of my own military service – as a young naval helicopter pilot – in the 1970s at an exercise area in the middle of nowhere, which somewhat inaptly took its name from the local town of Blissville.'

'As the father of two serving sons in the armed forces, who seem to have become hereditary helicopter pilots, I am greatly looking forward to talking to members and veterans of Her Majesty's Canadian armed forces... and to recognize their particular form of service to the nation,' he told the distinguished gathering.

Charles & Camilla's Tour

Prince Charles and the Duchess of Cornwall began their visit by celebrating Victoria Day in Toronto (always the Monday nearest 24 May, Queen Victoria's birthday) and enjoying an impressive lakeside fireworks display.

The following day, the Prince met university students, entrepreneurs (below), and Olympic athletes. He also met Dalton McGuinty, premier of Ontario and the Lieutenant-Governor David Onley, and he helped present the Lieutenant-Governor's Diamond Jubilee medals, awarded for community service. Then, for Prince Charles a visit to meet Olympic and Paralympic medal winners and athletes, while the Duchess of Cornwall enjoyed talking to soldiers and their families, and laid a wreath at the Memorial Wall. The Prince of Wales also met and accepted a feather (right), from Shawn Atleo, wearing a splendid traditional headdress in his capacity as National Chief of the Assembly of First Nations.

During their trip Prince Charles took part in a game of street hockey in New Brunswick and the couple played wooden spoons and drums with a music group, joined in a cookery class and listened to schoolchildren reading aloud. They also presented certificates at a citizenship ceremony (below right). Last stop on their tour was Regina, Saskatchewan, where they visited First Nations University.

Meanwhile the British were given a taste of Canada as the men and women of the Royal Canadian Mounted Police became the first foreign non-military unit to guard The Queen at Horseguards Parade, in London, during the changing of the Life Guard ceremony on 23 May. Stetsons replaced plumed helmets and lances rather than swords were carried, as the brave Mounties took over this traditional duty for one day, to mark the Diamond Jubilee. It was one of the rare occasions when Her Majesty has been guarded by both men and women.

The Queen's Family

The Queen and the Duke of Edinburgh have developed an extraordinary partnership in both their public and private lives during 65 years of marriage. Prince Philip, who gave up a brilliant naval career when his wife became Queen, has not only supported her in her royal duties but also worked hard himself, becoming patron or president of more than 800 organizations, overseeing the efficient running of royal residences, promoting British business interests and championing his Duke of Edinburgh Award scheme. The Queen frequently acknowledges her husband's role as her 'constant strength and guide' and together they are a formidable team.

Their four children and, now, their grandchildren, all support the 'Family Firm', undertaking visits at home and abroad, heading charitable organizations and acting as ambassadors for their country and the monarchy.

Each has made his or her mark. Heir to the throne, Prince Charles is a champion of the arts, music and environmental causes. He and Camilla, Duchess of Cornwall oversee the work of the Prince's Trust.

The Princess Royal, Princess Anne, is, like her mother, an excellent horsewoman, a former International Eventing champion who, in 1976, won a place in the British Olympic team. She is President of the British Olympic Association and undertakes around 600 annual engagements. In 2012, the year that London hosted the Olympic Games, Princess Anne travelled to Athens with David Beckham, Lord Coe and Boris Johnson to bring the Olympic Flame back to British soil before it started its relay journey to London. She carried the flame off the gold-painted British Airways flight 2012 when it landed at RAF Culdrose, in Cornwall.

Prince Andrew and Prince Edward also play a full part in the public duties of the Royal Family.

The newest family team is that of the Duke and Duchess of Cambridge, Prince William and his wife Catherine, who are taking on their share of duties, including a Jubilee visit to Malaysia on behalf of The Queen.

However, it is to The Queen and Prince Philip, at the head of the Royal Family, that the eyes of the nation and the world in this Jubilee year have turned with admiration, pride and a sense of celebration.

Photographs are reproduced by kind permission of Getty Images and Press Association.
Publication in this form copyright © Pitkin Publishing 2012.
Text copyright © Pitkin Publishing 2012.
Simultaneously published by Pitkin Publishing in the United Kingdom and Dundurn Press
in Canada.

Library and Archives Canada Cataloguing in Publication

Bullen, Annie
The Queen's Diamond Jubilee Year : A Royal Souvenir / Annie Bullen.

ISBN 978-1-4597-0835-8

1. Elizabeth II, Queen of Great Britain, 1926—Anniversaries, etc. 2. Elizabeth II, Queen of
Great Britain, 1926—Travel. 3. Queens—Great Britain—Biography. I. Title.

DA590.B84 2012   941.085092   C2012-903436-3

Printed and bound in Canada.
www.dundurn.com

Dundurn
3 Church Street, Suite 500
Toronto, Ontario, Canada
M5E 1M2

Dundurn
2250 Military Road
Tonawanda, NY
U.S.A. 14150